INTRODUCING
JOY

INTRODUCING
JOY

EVIDENCE OF VICTORY
FROM THE INSIDE OUT

CAROL SPEAR

Copyright © 2020 by Carol Spear. All rights reserved.

Printed in the United States of America

Editorial work by: Ellena Balkcom,
Written on Purpose Communications

Publishing services by Selah Publishing Group, Bristol, Tennessee. The views expressed or implied in this work do not necessarily reflect those of Selah Publishing Group.

No part of this publication may be reproduced, stored in a retrieval system or transmitted in any way by any means, electronic, mechanical, photocopy, recording or otherwise, without the prior permission of the author except as provided by USA copyright law.

ISBN: 978-1-58930-317-1
Library of Congress Control Number: 2020912603

DEDICATION

This book is dedicated to my Mom, the late Louise Mallory Gaulden. This lady encouraged and supported me in every endeavor. She would have been my PR person and largest marketer. I am truly grateful for her love and direction. She received the Joy of the Lord as a young woman and raised my sister, Christina Gaulden Newman, and I to know that "This Joy I have, the world didn't give it and the world can't take it away."

Table of Contents

Dedication 5
Acknowledgments 7
Introduction 9
Chapter 1
   Joy in Sorrow 13
Chapter 2
   Joy in the Final Days 19
Chapter 3
   Joy in Trouble 33
Chapter 4
   Joy in Depression 41
Chapter 5
   Joy in Revival 55
Chapter 6
   Joy in Forgiveness 69
      Epilogue 81

ACKNOWLEDGMENTS

I want to thank God and the Holy Spirit for giving me inspired writing to encourage and bless the readers. Without Godly inspiration, this project could never have been completed.

I want to thank my husband, Tommy, Maximos, our son, and my sister Christina Newman, for listening to every rough draft, edit, and final copy. Their love and encouragement have been extremely instrumental in completing this endeavor.

This book is a piece of fiction blended with true accounts of loved ones. I want to thank my uncle, Willie Mallory, who shared his version of family details with me after my mother's transition.

I want to thank my editor, Ellena Balkcom, who doubled as my editor and my accountability partner to get this work completed.

Finally, I want to thank the readers. May God richly bless you and may Joy abound in every area of your life.

INTRODUCTION

Please allow me to introduce myself. I am Joy. Many people think I am a feeling of great pleasure and happiness. This is incorrect. Feelings are an emotional state or reaction, which are directly embedded, ingrained or implanted within the flesh or our earthly perspective. Feelings or moods can come and go or change drastically, depending on our external circumstances. If I were to define myself, however, I would have to do it by my essence, for I am a spirit. If I were a directive, *be glad*, *be well*, *thrive*, and *rejoice* would define my very nature. Biblically, I am a 'Fruit of the Spirit.' Have you ever read or heard the scripture, "Taste and see that the Lord is good;" (Psalm 34:8)? Just as physical fruit nourishes the body with potassium and other important vitamins and minerals, spiritual fruit nourishes the soul. The entire scripture in Psalm 34:8 states, "Taste and see that the Lord is good; blessed is the one who takes refuge in him." As God is Spirit, so am I. Physically, you can't see me, but God can open your spiritual eyes to get a glimpse of what I might look like in your heart. I have several people I am

INTRODUCING JOY

going to interact with over the course of these pages. Each of them needed my essence to conquer areas in their lives that were overwhelming. As they share their stories with you, a clearer picture of me and why God sends me should be revealed. The bible tells you in the book of Nehemiah, "For the joy of the Lord is your strength." (Nehemiah 8:10) As you read each story, you will discover how I empower and give the strength of the Lord to His believers so that they may be overcomers, more than conquerors. My mission is to give them victory over their inner struggles and an outward display of my essence. Open your mind and your heart, as you continue reading. Embrace each story, learn the lessons ordained for you to apply to your life and encourage the characters in your spirit, as they first lean to their own understanding during their journey to discovering me. Everyone has access to a hidden jewel or treasure, but they have to know the location, possess the map, or have the key to unlock and possess the treasure. I am more precious than a jewel, more valuable than land and money. I am Joy, and I'm very pleased to meet you!

CHAPTER 1
JOY IN SORROW

My name is Mack, and I am fifteen years old. I am the oldest of seven brothers, and we live in a small two-family house in New York. As you can imagine, a household filled with rambunctious boys was loud and lively. My mom and dad have been married for sixteen years, and dad drives a truck for a living. Mom takes care of me and my younger brothers. Her job is extremely challenging. Cooking, cleaning, washing and running around after all of us is not easy. Today I found out that Mom is more than just tired; she is sick with a disease that has no cure. They call it incurable. I call it a mistake. The doctor must have mixed up mom's medical records and test results with someone else's. My mom is funny, young, wonderful and loving. She just needs some rest, that's all. I'll talk to my brothers about helping more and being quieter, so Mom can rest.

INTRODUCING JOY

My grandmother and my mom's sister come regularly to take Mom to her appointments with the doctor. On those days, I wait patiently on the front stoop for her to return from every doctor's visit. Each time I am hoping that the cure for this strange disease will be found, but I continue to be disappointed that nothing has changed. Mom and my grandmother have always made us attend church regularly. In our home, going to church was just as important as food. I remembered from my Sunday school class that prayer was our way to talk to God. I decided to talk to God about this situation with my mom.

"God, it's me, Mack. Sorry it's been so long since you've heard from me, and I know you are busy, but my mom needs you. They can't figure out what medicine to give her to make her well, but I know you can help. Please help the doctors, God, and help my mom. Thank you." As I got up from my knees, I felt that God had heard me and would heal my mom. I couldn't wait until the next appointment, so mom could tell me she felt like her old self again.

As time passed, I continued to pray and wait for the 'good report', as the older people say. The 'good report' never came, and one morning in July, my mom died. My mom is DEAD. I couldn't believe it…this had to be a bad dream. My mom is not even that old; she is thirty-five years old! Mothers are not supposed to die at thirty-five! I will never hear her voice singing in the choir, yelling at us to be quiet, or telling us to stop fighting. She will never again say *I love you, Son*. MY MOMMY IS GONE! Everyone says she's gone to Heaven, but what is that really? Where is it and can I visit her there? Am I an orphan now? Well, not really. I technically do still have my dad and brothers,

JOY IN SORROW

but what does life look like without Mom? They told me prayer works. They lied! I can't depend on anybody but myself now. I just want my mom back!

A few months after the funeral, my brothers and I moved in with my aunt and uncle. My dad continued to drive trucks and took on longer hauls for additional money. I think it was too hard for dad to consider finding a new job and raising seven boys, so this was the decision that was made FOR US. We had no say so, but we did have a loving family. One day close to the end of the summer, I noticed a girl visiting one of our neighbors. There was something about this girl. Not so much in how she looked, but something about her made me want to get to know her. She looked about my age, and I know she caught me staring at her. She had a friendly smile, and her eyes had a special sparkle in them. I didn't want to be teased by my brothers or have my interest misunderstood as a crush. I was determined to have a conversation with this girl before she returned home.

One evening as my brothers went riding with my uncle to get some ice cream, I purposely stayed behind just in case the neighbor's guest came outside. As I patiently sat on the front porch of our home waiting for her to come outside, my mind wandered back to the long evenings, sitting on the stoop, waiting for Mom to come home with that 'good report'. "What happened, God?" I thought. "Didn't you hear my prayers? Don't you care about us?" My heart was filled with sorrow, and I began to ache with grief and despair. The weight of sadness sat on my lungs, until I could barely breathe. As I gasped for air, the emotional roller coaster I was on screeched to an abrupt halt as

INTRODUCING JOY

a sweet voice said, "Hello." I looked up quickly and there she was standing right in front of me.

"Hello", I blurted. "My name is Mack."

"Yes, I know. I was sent here to meet you. My Father knows all about you and knew that you would need me today."

Puzzled, I looked at her closer to see if I had met her before.

"I don't know your father; I don't even know you," I said with both curiosity and irritation.

"Sure, you do. You see, I am Joy and my Father is God. Yeah, that God," she smiled as she rolled her eyes up and tilted her head up towards the setting sun.

"Months ago, you asked God to help the doctors and help your mom. He heard you and wanted to, but since He knows what's best and can't go against His own will, He did what was best, according to His knowledge. He knew that your mom was in a lot of pain and loved you boys so very much. Some refer to me as a 'Fruit of the Spirit'. All that really means is that when someone loves God, and their heart suffers deep sadness, grief or trouble due to the worries of life, I am sent to fill them with Joy from God. It's ok to miss your mom and question God for answers to impossible situations. God knows sorrow and grief, too. Jesus, the son of God, was deeply grieved when He knew a close friend named Lazarus would die. God Himself loved you, your family, and the entire world so much that He

JOY IN SORROW

sent his very own son, Jesus, to die for all of you. The true 'good report' is how determined God was to make sure that believers like Lazarus, your mom, and even you, one day would have a place for your spirit to live forever. He was so determined that He let His only begotten son die for the world. Heaven is the home God has created for those who love Him, and yes, it is a real place. There you live in the spirit, so you can't visit in your current form or flesh, as you questioned. However, you can rejoice in knowing that without this earthly body, there is no more sickness and no more death. In Heaven, you can rejoice and be glad just for being in the very presence of God. The *good report* of God is that His love for you is so deep that he sent His Holy Spirit to come and live in your heart. God knew that your heart would get very sad, and you would begin to think you were all alone, but He sent me to remind you of how special and how precious you are to Him. I'm here to give you an eternal joy, to have you experience great pleasure and delight in knowing that God loves you and is with you always. God Himself is the occasion for Joy. He *is* the 'Good News', and He is fair and favorable towards you. He causes you to be well and thrive. Your mom is with Him now, and she has no pain, only great joy."

My eyes were filled with tears and the lump in my throat was the size of a baseball. I was *not* alone, and I was *not* orphaned, after all. It was okay to miss my mom. Thank you, God, for taking care of Mom and sending me your Joy to let me know she is with you, filled with joy and out of pain. As I wiped my eyes and tried to refocus on Joy, she was gone, but her presence filled my heart and soul.

INTRODUCING JOY

SCRIPTURE FOR REFERENCE:

"In his neck remaineth strength, and sorrow is turned into joy before him."

(Job 41:22 KJV)

JOYFUL QUESTION:

How has God shown up for you in the midst of mourning or great sorrow, even when you prayed for a different outcome?

JOYFUL AFFIRMATION:

I will each day lean on *you* and not my own understanding. You are my rock and fortress, and I trust that my joy will be restored with each new morning.

CHAPTER 2
JOY IN THE FINAL DAYS

I see so much life in my firstborn child. He is a real jokester. He loves to play tricks on his brothers and has an infectious laugh that makes you double over with laughter just listening to him. I see how he mentors his younger brothers and tries to put on a brave face for their sake when things get challenging, but I can see the fear and concern that lies underneath. I'm noticing that his bright smile is getting dim. I'll need to address this soon.

My name is Polly, a silly name that my siblings dubbed me with as a child. I LOVED popsicles, and every weekend we would stop by the store and I would request a popsicle. My younger brother would chant, "Polly wants a popsicle, Polly wants a popsicle!" Well, as you can tell, the name stuck. I grew up in the rural area of Pittsylvania county, Virginia. My mom is an avid, dedicated Christian who insists that we are active in our local church. I always felt at home in the church and was keenly aware of the

INTRODUCING JOY

Spirit of God. My mom and her sisters often told me that I had a special anointing on my life. Back then, if a child was born with a thin layer of skin across her face, they referred to it as the "veil". Old wives' tales said that the person born with the veil was able to see into the spirit world. I remember my younger sister, Buey (Boo-ee) would sometimes get spooked by the conversation or reference, but I was comfortable in my own skin, no pun intended (smile). I gave my life to Christ and believed in God at a very early age. I was able to "see" things that no one else could. I remember one evening my mom asked us to take some oil to a neighbor who was in need. It was almost dusk, so Buey and I decided to cut through a field, which would save us some time. As we were walking through the field on the way home, I clearly saw two women crossing in the path mere feet from my sister and I. I remember pushing my sister aside saying, "Move over, Buey, you're going to run right into those two ladies." Of course, my sister thought I was kidding, but as we got older, she believed me and would get spooked. She never saw what I could, but that did not negate what I saw. I knew that I had a special gift, so I embraced it and sought God to help me understand why I had it and its usefulness to what He had planned for me.

I met my husband JR when I was 15 years old at Ebenezer Church. A mutual friend of some kids I knew, introduced me to a handsome guy named JR. He was a few years older than me, and I noticed he started coming around regularly. Back then we referred to dating as courting. A year after meeting JR, he planned to enlist in the military and wanted to marry me before he left for Kentucky. My dad was a very wise man. Educated in the state of New Jersey and twenty years older than my mom, Daddy called JR and I to the parlor or living room one evening to sit down and discuss the matter. Daddy posed his first question to me, "Polly, do you love him?" "Yes, sir, I do," I stammered. "JR are you prepared to love and take care of my daughter?" JR confirmed by saying, "Yes sir, Mr. Mallory. I give you my word." My mom chimed in, "You know Polly is underage and our consent is needed for you two to marry. I'll agree to consent if Polly stays home until you return for your first leave, or she turns of age." My daddy was in agreement with the marriage, but he made sure to let JR know that he wouldn't tolerate any foolishness concerning me and would gladly bring me home and deal with JR if he had to. Those were the terms, take it or leave it. JR looked at me with a little apprehension, but he knew negotiating was out of the question. We both agreed to the terms and we were married one weekend before JR had to report to Kentucky.

In the early years of our marriage, things were good. It turned out that JR's temper was too volatile or unpredictable for the military, and he wasn't keen on following directions. The discharge was amicable or agreeable to both parties, it turned out. JR worked hard, and we stayed on the land my parents worked on. Back then most black people were sharecroppers. They worked the land in order to live on it for a reduced price. My firstborn came into the world when I was 17 years old. Back in those days, poor women were not taken to the hospital, they used mid-wives to help with the delivery of a child. I remember being at home when my water broke and Momma running over telling Buey to call for Ms. Sally, the mid-wife, and tell her to hurry. The labor was hard and long, but it was all worth

INTRODUCING JOY

it when I saw the face of our son. JR and I decided to name him Mack. He was a beautiful, healthy baby, and I was so happy to be his mom. As a young mother, I was thrilled to have my family close by. My in-laws lived a little distance from us, so I didn't see them too much. A year later, I was expecting our second son.

I spent a lot of time taking in ironing for people and sewing when I could get the work to contribute to the income for our family. JR worked in the transportation industry and drove trucks for a living. This made it especially wonderful to live so close to my family. I always loved gospel music, so I was active in our church and sang in the choir. My reputation for singing was well known in our little area. When I sang praises and worshipped God in song, I was transported into His very presence. I sang until my soul was happy. I gave everything I had in every note and lyric that came out of my mouth. I envisioned the notes rising to the heavens, past the angelic hosts to the very throne of God. Sometimes I would get so caught up in worship that I needed an usher or choir member to touch me to bring me back into the confines of the church service. Yes, I loved the Lord.

In 1956 my parents moved to New York. My dad had two sisters who lived in New Jersey, and he wanted to give my younger siblings a better start in life. I worried what life would be like with my family moving so many hundreds of miles from me. I began to talk to JR about what our future looked like remaining in Virginia with a smaller support system for a family of five. By now I had three small sons. JR respected my dad and I could tell

JOY IN THE FINAL DAYS

that he was pondering the next steps he would make for our family.

We moved to Spring Garden, Virginia, a few months after my parents moved to New York. JR had some family that lived in the area, and we thought it was time for our boys to be around more children. The small home we rented had three large rooms which allowed the boys to comfortably share a room. I continued to take in piecework, ironing and sewing, in my new area. The strangest thing began to happen to me around this time. I began to see visions of heaven. The interesting thing was that I wasn't looking up into heaven, instead I was in heaven looking down on Earth. I remember praying about this vision, asking God to give me clarity and revelation concerning this. My answer was not in my immediate future. After nine months, JR decided it was time for us to visit my parents in New York. I was so excited, even more excited than the boys, I believe. I couldn't wait to see my momma and listen to my daddy share his stories. JR decided that we'd stay for a week, which would give him time to look around for possible job prospects. I knew in my knowing, my heart, that New York would be my next home.

When we arrived in Manhattan, New York, I was like a kid in the toy store with no limits on what I could have. I wanted to take it all in, as we drove through the tunnels and over the bridges. When we finally hit Westchester county, I understood why my parents chose New Rochelle to call home. Unlike the concrete jungle of skyscrapers and massive crowds, this area had tree-lined streets with parks and churches and children playing in front yards. I loved it. My parents had a me-

INTRODUCING JOY

dium sized two-story home with a large front porch. It sat on a corner lot with plenty of space in the yard for my boys to play safely. When we pulled up, my daddy beat my momma down the stairs and into the yard to welcome us. We hugged for what seemed like an eternity, as my sister swung Mack around and around. We were all united again, and all of us were thrilled.

June-bug, my baby brother, took JR around and introduced him to several of the guys who had moved from Virginia, North Carolina, and Georgia. A lot of the guys loved to hang out at our home and listen to daddy share wisdom and jokes. JR had some relatives who lived in Queens who we went to visit while we were in town. Every night Buey, Momma and I would sit on the porch for hours talking and reminiscing. I shared with them that I was pregnant again and felt it could be a girl this time. Buey expressed her concern that I was putting my body through trauma having my babies so close together. Momma assured her that women have been having babies every nine months for centuries, and I was a healthy and very fertile young woman.

The drive home was electrifying. All JR and I could talk about was the possibilities of raising our children in New York. His relatives in Queens had encouraged him to leave Virginia and said that they would help him find work. All I could think about was giving my boys a better life and opportunities to grow up with family and future cousins once Buey and June-bug married and had children. It was 1957 and I was 24 years old. I was ready to close this chapter of my life and begin a new one in a new place.

JOY IN THE FINAL DAYS

We moved in the Spring of 1958 to New Rochelle, New York. Momma and Daddy insisted that we stay with them until JR found a job and had several months of income saved up. Buey was working and courting a little go-getter from Georgia at that time, while June-bug was courting a pretty young lady from Martinsville, Virginia. JR found work right away and adjusted immediately to life in New York. Momma and Buey attended different churches, but I ended up joining Union Baptist Church, where Buey attended. I loved the pastor and congregation and felt right at home there. I noticed though that my energy level was a lot lower than usual, even after a good night's rest. I also noticed that my joints were getting stiff for no apparent reason. I shrugged it off and attributed it to running after the boys and packing boxes for the move.

We found an apartment not far from my parents after five months. It was a small duplex, which was a home that was shared by two families. It didn't have a large yard, but it was decent and in a safe area. Buey would pick me up for choir rehearsal every Thursday evening, while my neighbor would watch the boys. JR was driving longer distances and would only come home two days per week. Momma would come by several days per week to see the boys and sit and chat. Albert had proposed to Buey, and believe it or not, June-bug had proposed to his girlfriend. We were planning two weddings to take place in less than six months.

In June of 1959, Buey married Albert, June-bug married Rebecca and I gave birth to our fourth son. My marriage to JR became strained over the next several years. It seemed that he was away from the family more often and com-

INTRODUCING JOY

plained that I was always tired. I did my best to keep the boys entertained when he was home and to cook special meals, but it never rendered the reactions I was hoping it would. I drew closer to the Lord during this time, especially after finding out that my dad's health was declining. Buey would pick me up and I'd spend more time with Daddy, trying to keep him uplifted and singing old favorites to him.

In December of 1961, my daddy transitioned to his final resting place. Buey took it very hard. She was very close to Dad, but she was grateful that he got to meet her firstborn daughter, who was four months old at the time of his death. June-bug became a father the day after Daddy died. That old vision of heaven came back to me. Was this the meaning of my vision, preparation for Daddy's passing? But, why was I in heaven looking down on Earth? I continued to pray, "Not my will Lord, but thy will be done. Make it plain, Lord."

By 1968 I had seven boys, two nieces from Buey and Albert and two nephews from June-bug and Becky. Momma was healthy, working and serving in the church. All was well. . . almost. I noticed that a butterfly rash had shown up on my left cheek. I could not explain where the rash came from, but in addition to the rash, I was having a lot more joint stiffness and the fatigue had increased. Buey, being observant and always acting like the caretaker, insisted that I see a doctor. She took me to an appointment where my symptoms were dismissed as normal for a young woman with seven boys and low iron. Iron pills were prescribed and some vitamin supplements. Over the course of the next month, my symptoms appeared to be getting worse, rather than better. Buey insisted that I see a better doctor. She made me an appointment with her coworker's brother, Dr. Kaplowitz. When I met Dr. Kaplowitz, he was very kind and took several vials of blood and x-rays. He never focused on my daily routines, how many children I had or felt the need to offer vitamins. He concentrated on getting lab results. He wanted to see me back in two weeks to talk about the lab results. I must admit, I did feel a lot more confident in his skills and approach than in the first doctor's.

Over the course of the coming weeks, I had another spiritual encounter. This time I was wide awake, and the house was quiet, as everyone had been asleep for at least an hour. I was sitting at the kitchen table prepping food for dinner the next day, when I noticed the figure of a woman standing near the sink. Our dog, Tuffy, started to growl and I shewed him, trying to quiet him from waking up the household. He scurried and curled up right behind my legs at the table. I looked back up towards the sink and the woman was still in place. I said, "Lord, who is this?"

"Hi Polly! I'm Joy. I have been with you for such a long time that I feel no real introduction is needed. I am a Fruit of the Holy Spirit, and I am here just to strengthen you during this physical battle that is being waged on your body. You have had a relationship with and faith in God since you were a little girl. You have always been aware of the spirit realm, and I'm here to let you know, you will win once this is all over."

"I have no concern for my well-being, Lord, but what about my children and my family?"

INTRODUCING JOY

"God already knows that your children will be loved and cared for by your mom and sister. Just as He has always made provisions, you know He cannot lie."

"So, the vision He gave me years ago was for me and about me?" I asked.

"Yes, that is true. God knows how pure your heart is and how much you love him. He wanted to prepare you, so you could prepare others. Follow His instructions and know that in the end, you win!"

I had an overwhelming peace come over me, and although I didn't know how much time I had left, I knew what I needed to do before that time came. I called Buey the next day and asked her to stop by after work. She agreed and I prayed that God would lead me in preparing my sister for my transition. When she came in, she immediately inspected me and asked if I was okay. I assured her that I was better today than I had been in years. I asked her to sit next to me and to just listen until I was finished. I recounted for her the vision that I had years ago about me looking down from heaven. I then told her about the encounter with Joy last night. My sister had tears running down her face, as she shook her head, *no*. I reminded her that I never play when it comes to the things of God and that I would not give up the fight, but I would always choose God's will over my own. I told her what an inspiration she had been to me and how proud I am of the woman and mother she had become. I told her to help JR and see that my boys are well cared for and would remember me. My youngest was five years old at the time. We cried and rocked and held each other until the peace I felt transferred to my sister.

JOY IN THE FINAL DAYS

When she stood to leave, I asked her to let me talk to Mom and to keep praying for God's will to be done.

The following week we went to see Dr. Kaplowitz, who notified me that the disease I had was called, *Lupus Erythematosus*. He explained that this was an incurable disease which can affect any organ in the body. He further explained that it was a complicated and unpredictable disease with symptoms ranging from muscle pains, fever, joint stiffness and extreme fatigue. I listened intently as Buey held my hand. I was neither fearful nor distraught. I asked him for a timeframe. He shared that it seemed to be a very aggressive case, so he could not see my body holding up longer than the next six months. As we walked out of the office, I asked Buey to take me to Momma's house. I needed to see her. When I entered Momma's house, she began to cry. The Holy Spirit had already prepared her for the report. I embraced her and just held her until she was ready to let go. We sat down, and like my conversation with Buey, I shared my experience with Joy. She wept some more before ensuring me that JR and my boys would be supported and loved. She praised God for his mercy and prayed that I would not suffer long.

JR was never a religious man, and so I shared with him what Dr. Kaplowitz said. He also held me and wept like a small child. I knew that he loved me and would be overwhelmed with the thought of raising seven young boys under the age of 17 without help. I assured him that Momma and Buey would support him concerning the boys and that everything would be alright. I asked him to look out for Mack and the three oldest, since they were more attached to me and had more history and time

INTRODUCING JOY

with me than my younger babies. The last conversation I needed to have was with my firstborn.

I sat on the porch the next day and waited for Mack to come home. I asked him to sit with me for a while, since I wanted to talk to him. I began by telling him how proud I was to be his mom and that I loved him beyond words. "Have you ever thought about why God created us?" I asked.

"Not really, Mom," he responded.

"Well, I think I was created to bring seven awesome sons into the world to change the world."

"Umm, ok if you say so," he responded.

"I know you are strong and brave, but I want you to always look out for your brothers and love God. Can you do that for me?"

He looked me in the eyes and said, "Sure, Mom. Can I ask you something to do for me?"

"Sure," I said.

"Don't ever leave us, Ok?"

"I am not in control of when I leave here, Mack. You understand that God is in control of everything, right, not me? I can promise you that everything will be alright, because He is in control as long as you follow Him. Is that okay with you?"

"I guess it will have to be," he said reluctantly. I pulled him into me and held him for the last time, with the same love I had for him when he was born.

JOY IN THE FINAL DAYS

On July 15th, at the age of thirty-five, I went home to be with the Lord. I thank God for my short time on Earth and the sons that I was assigned to bring here. I will miss each of them, but the JOY of the Lord was my strength until the end. Joy can be yours, as well, through all manner of sickness on this Earth and even until death. Jeremiah 29:11 says it best, "For I know the plans I have for you, declares the Lord, plans to prosper you and not harm you, plans to give you hope and a future." My future was to be with Him, in Heaven!

SCRIPTURE FOR REFERENCE:

"As the days wherein the Jews rested from their enemies, and the month which was turned unto them from sorrow to joy, and from mourning into a good day: that they should make them days of feasting and joy, and of sending portions one to another, and gifts to the poor."

(Esther 9:22 KJV)

JOYFUL QUESTION:

Can you think of a time when you have felt prepared by the Holy Spirit for trouble to come? How did it increase your peace and joy during that season?

JOYFUL AFFIRMATION:

No matter what is happening around me, I will take rest and refuge in you, my Father. Your joy will fill my Spirit, in all things and at all times.

CHAPTER 3
JOY IN TROUBLE

My mom has been sick with a mental illness all her life. What may seem simple to most, like choosing an outfit to wear for the day, may take her hours. There's no special occasion, big date, or job interview, but simply choosing an outfit to put on to sit in the house is a major time-consuming task. She loves me very much, but really doesn't know how to take care of a growing teenager. I need rules and boundaries, expectations and encouragement. These things are probably taken for granted in most households, but what if you grew up without them and was never exposed to a functional family that had these things in place. For my mom, determining what rules to set and what to expect from me is blurred in her picture of reality. She has never worked, due to her illness, and is content sitting at home drinking sodas and eating snacks, while watching her favorite television shows. This is enjoyment, no, contentment to her.

INTRODUCING JOY

My dad has another type of mental illness. He suffered a great loss in his life as a child, and as a result of that loss, he shut down mentally and began to medicate his depression with alcohol and drugs. He refused to grow up and mature to a fully functioning, independent man, so now at age thirty-eight, he lives the life of a perpetual victim. He sees himself as a failure and believes that his survival depends on the pity and handouts of others. Somewhere in his lifetime, he concocted a twisted plan for survival, which was to stay on the streets, do illegal drugs and alcohol, and recite a sad story to strangers before he begged them for money. He believed that our welfare system and the compassion of others would be his key to existence.

My parents love each other in their own way. My mom hates to be alone and my dad wants to be taken care of. I guess this dysfunction works for them and their co-dependency, and I guess their love brought me into this world. My name is Rachel, and I am thirteen years old.

My social worker decided one day that my mom really was unable to take care of me at this stage in my life. I was having some issues of being bullied at school, and I had anger issues when provoked. As a baby, I guess I was easier to handle. All she had to do was hold me, feed me and change me. I have aunts, uncles, and grandparents who have helped raise me over the years. It was the exposure to 'normal' family dynamics that illuminated the abnormality of my home. I am very smart and driven to have a different life for myself, a normal life. I am soft spoken and likeable, almost shy, but I rage when I am yelled at or feel opposed or threatened in any way. The other kids say I overdose, or 'OD', when I get angry. I just hate to be yelled at. I now

JOY IN TROUBLE

live in a group home for girls in Northern Michigan. I got here as a result of my anger and attitude. At first, I thought the group home would keep me for a night or two and send me home. It has been three months now, and I am planning to go 'AWOL'. That's what they call it here when you leave without permission or run away. I have cousins who live in Florida. I visited one summer, and it was great! All the kids were nice to me, and we went on all kinds of trips and did all sorts of neat things. That's where I am headed. I want to live with my cousins in Florida.

Every weekend there are several trips that the staff of St. John's plans for the girls. This weekend they are planning to take us to the Metroplex, which houses twenty theaters in one building. The Metroplex is downtown and the train stations are in walking distance. I have already looked up the train schedule on the internet, so I know exactly what time to leave the theater to catch the train. We earn weekly allowances at St. John's based on behavior. I have saved all of my money and currently have $118 on account. I have enough to buy a one-way ticket and a meal. "I am outta' this place in six more days," I thought. As the days passed, I found myself more and more excited and self-confidence emerged. "No one will tell me where to live," I thought. If I can get to Florida, I will be happy and can come back to Michigan, once I am grown.

Today is my big day! I rolled up five of my favorite outfits and banded them with a rubber band. I hid them in my backpack along with my money. I put on my favorite sneakers and happily got on the van headed to the Metroplex. "Bye-bye, St. John's," I thought as the van rolled out of the gates. I purposely choose a movie that no one else

INTRODUCING JOY

wanted to see. I have a good reputation with the staff and had earned their trust. They agreed to let me watch the movie I chose and I promised to meet back at the concession stand as soon as the movie was over. About halfway through the movie, I quickly walked out exaggerating my walk with a drink in my hand, as if I had waited too long to use the restroom. As I hopped across the lobby and into the restroom, I quickly changed into another outfit and put my hair up in a baseball cap. I walked confidently straight out the side door of the Metroplex and never looked back. I walked swiftly about five blocks, before I turned around to see if anyone had followed me. "Wow, that was easy!" I said to myself. "Those people are so stupid; I should have done this weeks ago!" As I focused on my surroundings and what street I was on, I made my way to the subway station, which would take me to the bus station. Daylight is just beginning to set, which meant it would be dark soon. I had taken the subway with my mom before, so I knew how to buy my token and which platform to stand on. According to the subway map, my stop is three stops away. As the train rolled into the station, I noticed that several lights on this platform were broken. No one was waiting to get on, and I seem to be the only passenger getting off. I felt uncomfortable and considered staying on the train, but I was determined to see my plan through to the end. Apprehensively, I stepped off the train and onto the platform. The silence was noticeably eerie. It reminded me of a scene from a horror movie where the main character knows she should not be somewhere, but blindly, she continues in the wrong direction. Quickly, I walked through the turnstile and out into the night air.

JOY IN TROUBLE

Once I was on the street, I could smell urine and burning trash. Several people were out, but no young girls or women. Rough looking boys with too much time on their hands and too little money in their pockets were gathered in packs. Old men gripping whiskey bottles and beer cans huddled near fences of dilapidated buildings. I kept my head up and my eyes focused straight ahead as I walked with determined steps past them. A few tried to get my attention by yelling out, "Hey girl, can I go with you?" and "You got any change to spare?"

I ignored the noise and never stopped or answered. I was on my way to Florida. As I turned the corner and spotted the bus station, I smiled with a great feeling of accomplishment. I CAN do anything I put my mind to, just like my aunt told me years ago. I put my plan into action and was now walking into the bus station. As I purchased my one-way ticket and sat on the wooden bench, I realized that I was hungry. I saw vending machines close by, so I walked over to buy some snacks for the long ride. I noticed several girls sitting on a bench close to the vending machines. Some looked around my age, but most were older. As I walked up and bought my snacks, I noticed that the girls ended their conversations. I decided to use the restroom before the bus came. I ignored the stares and put my snacks in my backpack and walked into restroom. Within seconds of stepping into the restroom, I felt blows pelting me like dense sleet on an icy day. The punches were coming from all directions. My head was spinning, and I could taste my own blood in my mouth, as someone's fist smashed my nose. Through the tears and blood, I fought with all my might. I know I hurt some of them, but there were far too many for me to effectively defend myself. I felt

INTRODUCING JOY

my sneakers being ripped off my feet, my backpack straps were cut and easily lifted from me. When it was all over, I rolled over to find my clothes torn; sneakers, ticket, money and backpack gone. Never had I felt such rage, fear and danger. I crawled into a stall and cried out to God. "Why did you do this to me? I've always tried to be good, but I keep attracting trouble. Where are you and why don't you help me?" I yelled. I cried from the depths of my soul, not because of the physical pain I was in, but from the totality of the misfortune I have endured in my short lifetime. I heard the stall door open and a girl my age standing in front of me. Remarkably, I wasn't afraid and didn't think she was one of the crew who jumped me. Something about her eyes told me she was here to help me.

"Are you alright, Rachel? My name is Joy and I've been sent by God to help you in this time of trouble. You see I am sent as a result of your sincere prayer for help and your belief in God. Some refer to me as a 'Fruit of the Spirit'. All that really means is that I am sent to someone who loves God in their heart, but that is experiencing severe sadness, sorrow, or trouble. Your trouble didn't start tonight Rachel, but long ago when you decided to do things your way and disregard the warnings and wise counsel given to you. You were destined for trouble due to your choices. Your mental state and willfulness led you to this stall. Do you remember the nervousness you felt back on the train when you pulled into the station? That was the Holy Spirit trying to warn you to change your plans. Did you know that it was God's great love for you that caused your relatives to step in during the course of your life to nurture you and take you to church to make

JOY IN TROUBLE

sure you knew God and his teachings? It was His love that protected you when you got off the train and walked past all those men and boys who could have killed you for less than the things stolen from you. Those girls hurt your pride, body, and took material things that can be replaced and healed by God. It was God's mercy that kept your life from being taken. Trust that God loves you and has great things in store for you, Rachel."

The sound of the restroom door opening distracted me as I wiped the tears from my eyes. A woman entered with her little girl and saw me on the floor torn and bruised. Immediately she ran up to me and offered aid. I explained that I had been jumped and needed to contact someone at St. John's group home for girls. As I turned to look for Joy, I noticed she was no longer present. I returned to St. John's not ashamed or angry that my plan had failed, but with joy in my heart knowing God loved me and had spared my life. Through his Joy, I learned to trust God and let *Him* lead me to my purpose and destiny, rather than devising my own plans based on my will.

SCRIPTURE FOR REFERENCE:

"For I know the plans I have for you," declares the Lord, "plans to prosper you and not to harm you, plans to give you hope and a future."

(Jeremiah 29:11) (Esther 9:22 KJV)

JOYFUL QUESTION:

Think of a time when you had your plans set in stone, but God seemed to have a completely different plan. How did you respond then, and how would you respond differ-

INTRODUCING JOY

ently once it's clear to you that God is redirecting you for His own purpose?

JOYFUL AFFIRMATION:

God, your plan for me is perfect and was pre-ordained before I was formed in my mother's womb. I trust your Holy Spirit to guide and direct me in all things concerning my life.

CHAPTER 4
JOY IN DEPRESSION

I'm going to warn you ahead of time that you have to pay close attention when I'm speaking. My mind processes very quickly, but my speech is fragmented and a lot slower to my audience. It is very frustrating to see the confusion in the faces of the people I am talking to. Hell, they are supposed to be so much smarter than me, but they can't even follow a simple conversation. I apologize, my name is Quincy. Quincy John Stanton. I am my mother's baby boy. I have an older brother Dallas and a few stepbrothers from women my Pops dealt with. Dallas and I are my mother's only children. So, where should I start?

I was a very happy and active child, based on the accounts of Pops and my aunties. Who could ever imagine that a mosquito bite could alter your life forever? I have very few recollections of what happened to me back then. It's funny how accounts repeated to you over an extended period can blur or replace your own firsthand account.

INTRODUCING JOY

It really doesn't matter though. Too many relatives tell the same story, so it has become my account now as well. From what I've been told, I began to show signs of confusion and slumped into a routine of sleeping a lot. My Mom, Becky, immediately noticed that her lively baby boy was way too inactive. I seemed to have lost my appetite, and once my temperature spiked beyond 101 degrees, my Mom took me to the emergency room. The doctors determined that I showed signs of a bite, possibly a mosquito. They began sticking me with needles and taking blood samples. I remember it hurting, crying out for help to my parents, and not much after that. the doctors were trying to figure out how a six-year-old boy could be bitten in the suburbs of New York City by a mosquito carrying a disease similar to Malaria. I was diagnosed with *encephalitis* and was in a coma for months. I am told that my Mom, Pops, Gramma (Pops' mother), and aunties created a round-the-clock rotation to be at the hospital to support me. My Mom refused to leave my side. I woke up out of that coma on Sunday, April 6, 1969. My Mom and Gramma danced and praised God in that hospital room that day! God had answered their prayers and it was not a coincidence that I opened my eyes on Easter Sunday. This was extremely memorable to my family. My family is Christian and very rooted in their belief of God, Jesus, and the Holy Spirit. My Pops said my mother and grandmother, his mother, would pray fervently for hours every day for my healing and full recovery. The doctors said I would have to go through a lot of rehabilitation to regain my motor skills and speech. Once he was allowed to see me, Dallas asked me why I sounded so funny. Out of all the conversations I had, and all the things that were going on at that time, it is inter-

JOY IN DEPRESSION

esting that this was something that stuck with me. I don't know, maybe it's because he's my big brother.

I remember that once I was able to leave the hospital I had to go to a special school. It was called Sunshine College and located in upstate New York. I later found out that this place treated and rehabilitated critically ill children. Eventually, I was released from Sunshine College and returned to public schools in my district. I had trouble initially fitting back in, but Dallas stood up for me. A lot of the families who lived in the same housing projects called me a miracle and said God had a calling on my life. I don't know about that, but I wouldn't debate them openly. I was just happy to be home.

Over the course of the next two years, my Mom and Pops began to argue more. As a nine-year old kid, I didn't understand the depth of the arguments until one day when my Mom decided to pack me and my brother's things. We understood that we were going to visit our Memaw (Memawh), my mother's mom. We enjoyed traveling south to Virginia and looked forward to seeing our grandparents, aunties and other cousins. I'll never forget the day when one of my aunts wanted Mom to attend a baseball game with her. It was an old high school rival game, but more like a reunion of some of her old classmates. I understood that my aunt was really trying to cheer my Mom up and wanted to get her mind off of the situation with my Pops. I remember that they were gone for about three hours before the call came in and my Memaw started screaming. We could hear her through the open kitchen window facing the back of the house. Dallas and I were out back playing with our cousins and some neighborhood kids. We all ran

INTRODUCING JOY

into the house to find my Memaw on the floor screaming, "No! No! It can't be!" One of my aunties had the phone and was weeping hysterically. Dallas and I just looked at each other, wondering what had happened. We were all shooed back outside and told we would talk later. A lady from the neighborhood came over about thirty minutes later and asked us to come and play with her children at her house. She tried to bribe us by saying she had just baked a hot apple pie and was going to pick up some ice cream on the way home. Our auntie told us to go with the lady and that she would be over to pick us up a little later. I had no idea what to think and neither did Dallas. "What's wrong?" I asked. She promised to explain later, so Dallas and I walked along in silence with the lady three houses down. I remember it seemed to take a lot longer than it should.

Later that night my Aunt Dora showed up at the lady's house to bring us to Memaw's house. Her eyes were red and swollen like she had been stung by yellow jackets. Dallas asked, "Aunt Dora, what happened?" I chimed in and said, "Yeah, and where's Mom?" It looked like it took all of Aunt Dora's strength to climb the three steps to the front door. Memaw had a swing on her front porch and two rocking chairs. Aunt Dora was Mom's baby sister. "Come sit with me boys," she said as she slumped down on the swing. Dallas and I sat next to her and squinted to see her face closely in the light of the moon and the yellow porch light. "A terrible thing happened at the game this afternoon boys. Some people had too much to drink and started arguing. Before your mom and I had a chance to leave, someone started shooting," she explained. Her voice began to break up as tears streamed down her face.

JOY IN DEPRESSION

Dallas and I listened intently. "Before we could get up and leave, a bullet hit your Mom in the chest," she wept. Dallas began crying and I sat there for a minute trying to process what she said. "So, what hospital is she in? Take us to see her!" I demanded while motioning to stand. Aunt Dora wrapped her arms around both of us and said, "Boys, she's not in the hospital. The gunshot killed her right there in the bleachers. I am so sorry." Dallas crumbled into the arms of Aunt Dora at that very moment. "Liar! You're a liar!" I screamed as I ran out to the road as fast as I could. I had no idea where I was going, but I knew my mom was not dead. "I can't believe Aunt Dora would say something stupid like that," I thought to myself. Aunt Dora screamed to my uncle to run and catch me. When he caught up to me, I had made it about half a mile. He scooped me up from behind and dropped down on his knees. He too was weeping as he held me close and muttered, "I'm so sorry," over and over again. My head was now pounding as hard as my heart was beating. I remember punching my uncle in his chest and arms as I yelled, "Liar! You are all liars!" This was the last thing I remember before fainting.

The next day I awoke in Memaw and Papa's bed. I overheard Aunt Dora saying to my aunts in New York that the paramedics came out and every time they revived me, I would try and fight them. Eventually, they gave me and Dallas a mild sedative to get us through the night. "Good morning boys. I have some lunch ready for you. Do you want to come to the table?" Aunt Dora asked. Dallas and I silently walked to the kitchen and sat down. My head started pounding all over again. "Your dad is on the road and should be here by this evening," she said. "Is it true, Aunt Dora? Was Mom really killed at the game?" asked

INTRODUCING JOY

Dallas. I could feel myself ready to explode. "How dare he believe these liars?" I fumed! "Unfortunately, it is true, Dallas," whispered Aunt Dora. "It all happened so fast. One minute we were laughing and talking and the next minute, people were screaming and running as shots rang out. I remember turning to Becky to say let's go, but she was holding her chest and then ... it was too late. It was too late," she wept. Dallas was crying all over again, but not me. I would not believe it until I saw my Mom.

Dad must have broken every speed limit between New York and Virginia. He burst into Memaw's house and yelled our names. We ran to him and jumped in his arms. This was the first time I remember seeing my dad cry. He squeezed us so tight that I thought our ribs would be crushed. My aunties and Memaw rescued us from the death grip and brought dad something to eat. Aunt Dora recounted the story all over again, as my uncle stood guard at the door, prepared should I sprint out again. Dad explained to us that he would take us to the funeral home once all the arrangements had been made. He assured us that everything would be alright, in time. I wonder why people say such stupid things during death. There is no comfort in words at that time. True to his word, two days after his arrival, we got in the car and headed to the funeral home. I remember driving up to this huge white house with black trim. Men in black suits were standing on the porch to greet us. As we walked up to the door, I could feel my heart pounding to the point that I could hear my heartbeat in my ears. My Pops bent down and said to both of us, "Be strong, boys. You know your Momma loved us. I'm right here with you." We were led by one of the men adorned in a black suit down the hall to an open room. I immediately spotted the

JOY IN DEPRESSION

casket, front and center of the room. As we slowly walked up to the casket, Pops held each of our hands. The closer we got to the casket the more Dallas began to whimper. I studied my Mom's face when I got close enough. Her eyes were shut and hair combed just like she wore it when she came from Ms. Lewis' shop. Her lips had a slight smile and her arms were folded across her stomach. I just stared for what felt like days, yet mere minutes, trying to find some flaw that would prove *this was not my Mom*. When Pops touched my shoulder, it was like a trigger that shot me out of a cannon. I screamed out and tried to jump into the casket. My Pops grabbed me just before I would've tumbled the casket or landed on top of my Mom. All denial and anger combusted like a toxic gas, as I faced the reality that my Mom was gone. My dad had me curled up in his arms like a barbell as he scurried out of the room with me. Conversations and words of sympathy were all a fog during the few days that followed. We attended the funeral, and once again, I wanted to get in the casket with my Mom. I literally wanted to die with her. In my mind, I retreated to a safe place and began to relive the days and weeks after I woke up from the coma. I would wake up every day to Mom sitting in a chair next to my bed, smiling at me. I was her Quincy. I was her baby boy. She would read books to me, make me laugh, and hold my hand for hours, day after day. If my Mom was in heaven like everyone said, then I was surely heaven bound.

As the weeks and months passed, I remember returning to New York and living with my Pops and Dallas in our apartment. My Gramma and aunts made sure we had cooked meals, activities, and were cared for while my Pops worked. I eventually started acting out in school. I began

INTRODUCING JOY

having hallucinations of my Mom standing outside of the classroom or across the street. I would run out and try to get to her before the vision was gone. Several of these attempts put me physically in danger of being hit by a car or bus. The school psychiatrist began meeting with me weekly and my Pops was constantly called to the school because of my behavior. I was prescribed anti-depressants and other psychological meds. One night I was at the home of my aunt Buey and everyone was bustling around the house. Adults were outside playing cards on the porch, and my cousins were across the street in the field playing tag and catching fireflies. I remember my Mom telling me to come to her. She directed me to the guest room, and no one noticed me slip upstairs. There was a light fixture on the wall, which Mom told me to pull off the wall and grab the wire. I remember pulling the fixture with all my strength, as all the lights in the house went off. Someone ran into the room and grabbed me up before I could touch the live wire. Gramma and my aunts said I was yelling incoherently, "Mom wants me to come to her. I have to get to Mom. Let me go!" This was the last incident I remember in my childhood before I was taken to the hospital to be reevaluated. My Pops believed that the encephalitis from years ago had caused brain damage and that I needed additional help.

Over the next twenty years, I struggled with drug addiction and alcoholism. Life never gave me a break after my Mom died. I had a supportive family and my Pops was only thirty years old when she died, so women were all over him. My Pops is very charming, tall, handsome and made a decent living as a bus driver. I didn't blame him for remarrying and moving on, but I could not. I dropped

JOY IN DEPRESSION

out of high school and struggled to hold down a job. My reality was too painful to stay sober. People have no idea what it is like to have periods of depression, confusion, and inner struggles. I remember meeting Sonya outside of the building she lived in. She was a pretty woman with one daughter. She seemed to understand me when I talked to her, and I understood she had some issues too. She was diagnosed with bipolar disorder and so was I. Unlike me she never did drugs or alcohol. The only time we would argue was when our disability checks came in at the first of the month. Instead of me giving her some funds to help keep the household going, I would buy alcohol and find a hit of whatever I could afford. Don't you dare judge me! This had nothing to do with choice, but the disease that I was trying to live with. My Gramma and aunts would try to talk to me about coming to church or family functions. The thing is, if I took one little nip, one little drink before I showed up for Christmas dinner, Thanksgiving, the birthday celebration, or whatever, they said I was so annoying they wanted me to just sit down and be quiet. Why the hell do you continue to invite me? You know if I have one drink and access to a second, I'm going to drink the beer until there are no more to be found. You know if I feel anxious, I might stop and get something to take the edge off before I come. Why are you frustrated or annoyed by me? This constant sober versus high battle eventually led me to stop coming to family functions.

Years after Mom passed, Dallas got strung out on crack and went to prison. He met a good girl and fathered the first baby girl in the family. While I had petty stunts with jail, I never did hard time due to my psychiatric records on file with the state. I was usually sent back to a facility

INTRODUCING JOY

upstate to detox for a number of weeks, or a few months maximum. When Sonya got pregnant with our daughter, Rachel, my family was thrilled. You see, my girl cousins didn't have any children, so Rachel was the second baby girl in the family. The real concern for Rachel was being brought up in a home with two dysfunctional people. Initially my Pop's sister, Buey, and her daughter would pick Rachel up on weekends and take her shopping and to church on Sundays. Eventually the concern turned to me taking Rachel out on the streets and telling her to dance for people, as I begged for money to help take care of her. Yeah, it was morally wrong, but those drug and alcohol demons were real. I loved my daughter and meant her no harm, but I saw how her cute little face and my sad story could work for my benefit. Sonya never questioned why I wanted Rachel to walk to the store with me or why I'd bring her back at different times, depending on the fruit of our labor. What did happen was family and friends who saw Rachel with me on the streets began reporting back to Aunt Buey or Pops. My cousin in Georgia was single and doing well, so she agreed with her Mom and sister that maybe getting Rachel out of the environment would give her a better chance to grow up in some normalcy. Sonya didn't fully understand but agreed to sign the papers giving my cousin custody in Georgia. I knew that this was meant to bless and help my daughter, but where the hell was all this support when I was growing up? Why didn't anyone think about my normalcy? Was it normal for a nine-year-old boy to have his mother shot and killed at a baseball game? Would they turn my daughter against me, or make her think she was better than me?

JOY IN DEPRESSION

Over the years, Rachel returned to New York and had her own struggles. Never with drugs or criminality, but definitely with self-love and esteem. She was willful, and I made sure to let her know she would end up like me and her mother. She wasn't better than us. She came from us! During one of my rants and ravings, Sonya said, "Why would you say that to her? What is wrong with you? You shouldn't talk to your daughter like that." Later that night I was walking home, taking a short-cut through a closed park. I really thought about what Sonya said. Why was I so angry at Rachel? What made me lash out at her? Fear came to mind. I don't fear my daughter. That's crazy, but was she ashamed of me? Would she grow up and want nothing to do with me? Feelings of self-pity and sorrow were sweeping over me. Tears began to stream down my face as I contemplated my failure as a father. "Lord, what have I done? I didn't mean what I said. I can't handle another loss. Please don't let me lose my daughter," I begged. I felt a sense of peace and clarity come over me. I could feel the presence of someone standing next to me. I slowly turned my head to see the figure of a person standing a few feet away. I strained my eyes under the park's lamp post to try and identify the person. I could tell that it was a woman, but I didn't know her.

"Quincy, it will be okay in the end."

"Who the hell are you?" I asked.

"My name is Joy, Quincy. I have been waiting to meet you for a long time."

"How do you know me?"

INTRODUCING JOY

"Quincy, I am the Fruit of the Holy Spirit. Joy manifests in the lives of people who are at their weakest point and who the Holy Spirit knows is ready for this encounter. You have a pure heart, Quincy, but it is locked under so many weights of this world. Years ago, when you were in a coma as a little boy, your Mom Becky and your family members petitioned God daily on your behalf. They loved you so much that they begged God not to take you from them. He honored their prayers and allowed you to live."

"Why allow me to live in a condition of hell? When I'm sober, I can't think. When I'm high, I'm useless. Who wants to live like this? Why didn't God just allow me to die with my Mom or after she died when I was younger?"

"Quincy, God gets no glory in using people who have it all together. He knew that mankind would NEVER have it all together, that's why He had to send His son, Jesus. The very illusion of having it all together is a trick of the enemy. God wants to use people like you and Rachel to give him glory. No one functions at 100 percent in this world. Your illness and brain damage does not exempt you from being used by God. You and Sonya brought a beautiful child of God into this world. Do you not see God's hand on her life? God used Jesse and his wife to father King David. He used Hannah and Elkanah to father Samuel, Jochebed and Amram to father Moses, and the list goes on and on. These people were not perfect, but God had a plain for their children to do great exploits in the Earth. Don't begrudge the favor of God on Rachel's life. Rachel loves you and doesn't blame you or hold grudges against you. She has a heart of compassion. Bless God and pray that you live to see the plan God has for her. He has one for you too, Quincy. God

JOY IN DEPRESSION

never left you and Dallas. He favored you as well to get the help you needed when you could not help yourself. Think of all the counseling and strategies you have been given. God put those people in place to equip you for war with depression and anxiety. Psalms 139:7-8 states, "Where can I go from your Spirit? Or where can I flee from Your presence? If I ascend into heaven, You are there; If I make my bed in hell, behold, You are there." There is no hiding from the presence of the Lord. Call upon Him in your darkest struggles. He will be the Light to lead you out of the pit of isolation, despair, and depression. You see, Psalm 139:13 states, "For You formed my inward parts; You covered me in my mother's womb." Quincy, praise God, for you are fearfully and wonderfully made. You matter! Accept His love and mercy, because truly His Grace is sufficient! "Be glad, be well, thrive, and rejoice!"

As I dropped my head to process the words she spoke, I felt strengthened and encouraged. "Thank you. Lord! Forgive my actions and hurtful words to Rachel. You know this is hard for me, but I can do better with your help. I remember being told to look to you for help and not drugs or alcohol. Help me conquer fear and not succumb to old habits when I am challenged by emotional battles. When I looked up again through tear-filled eyes, Joy was gone. Her task was complete, and I knew that I did matter to God, for greater is He that is in me!

SCRIPTURE FOR REFERENCE:

"For God hath not given us the spirit of fear; but of power, and of love, and of a sound mind."

(2 Tim 1:7 KJV)

INTRODUCING JOY

JOYFUL QUESTION:

We sometimes feel afraid, judged, dismissed, ashamed, anxious and just mentally unfocused or confused. Fear and confusion can distort your view of reality and make you feel defensive in a situation that doesn't warrant it. Has fear – lack of power, love or a sound mind – ever made you feel misjudged, misunderstood or made you unfairly judge or ostracize a loved one?

JOYFUL AFFIRMATION:

I am fearless because of the power and perfect love of Christ that dwells within me. I have a sound, transformed mind that is fixed on the things of God and joy replaces all fear, shame and confusion.

CHAPTER 5
JOY IN REVIVAL

I finally arrived at my aunt's home in the early morning hours. It had been an exhausting trip from Saudi Arabia to Atlanta. The air was thick and humid, and a full moon was setting in the clear sky. My aunt's home was very spacious and filled with every comfort I could imagine. As she directed me to my room, I hugged her quickly and immediately jumped into the large inviting bed against the far wall. I was way too tired to even consider how my life would change living in Atlanta. As I looked around the room, I slowly closed my eyes and allowed my body to surrender to the deep, peaceful sleep it longed for.

The warmth of the morning sun shone brightly through the window on my face. My family agreed to let me complete my senior year of high school and eventually attend college in the states. My family was one of the wealthier families in my area. and I had attended all of the top schools in my country. The opportunities my aunt

INTRODUCING JOY

wrote home about were too attractive for my family to ignore. She worked as a surgeon in one of the top hospitals in the Atlanta area and had purchased a home big enough for my entire family to relocate if they chose to. This area has schools with excellent reputations and top scholars. I would be tested and registered as a high school senior on Monday morning. All morning I unpacked and customized my room to suit my tastes. My aunt thought of everything, computer, television, gaming systems, etc. My new home had a large back yard with a privacy fence. I decided to take a stroll through the neighborhood, wondering if I might run into some other kids my age. As I walked down the manicured sidewalks, all I could see were tall privacy fences and security gates. "What's up with all the security?" I thought. This was not what I expected in the 'land of the free and home of the brave'. As I returned home, my aunt picked up on my disappointment.

"Don't feel too badly, Ahmir. I've lived here for six months, and due to my work hours, I haven't met anyone either. I'm sure when you start school Monday, you'll make friends quickly." I smiled and challenged my aunt to a game of ChessMaster on the PlayStation.

On Monday morning, I woke up before sunrise. I was eager to get to school and meet someone my own age. I put on my favorite jeans, a lightweight cotton shirt and sneakers. As the clock approached 8:00 a.m., my aunt and I drove onto the grounds of Northwick High School. The entrance exam was a breeze. I scored in the top 5 percent. Once I registered and received my class schedule, my aunt gave me money for lunch, a key to her house, and a detailed map of which bus to take at the end of the day. By the end of the day, I was disappointed that most of my classes were uneventful, and I had not made one new friend. As I boarded the bus home, I noticed there was only one seat left. I sat down next to a boy about my age and decided to introduce myself.

"Does this bus stop in the Magnolia sub-division?" I asked.

"Yeah. Is this your first day?" replied the boy.

"It is. My name is Ahmir, and I'm a senior. What grade are you in?"

"12th. Where are you from, Ahmir?"

"Saudi Arabia. What's your name?"

"Luke. Luke Barren. How was your first day at Northwick?"

"Okay, I guess. The work appears to be easy, but I just don't know many people yet."

"Well, this is my stop, Ahmir. See you around."

Luke got off the bus and disappeared behind an aisle of tall trees, which led to enormous homes from the glimpse I got as the bus rolled on. *At least I met one person today*, I thought. *Tomorrow, I'll plan to meet two and by the end of the week I hope to know at least ten new people.* When I got home, I was excited to tell my aunt that I met Luke. We didn't have much time together as she prepared to leave for the hospital. I reviewed my assignments, emailed my friends and family members back home and fell asleep.

INTRODUCING JOY

The next morning, I told my aunt I could take the bus to school. She worked all night, and there was no reason for her to take me to school every morning. She recognized my need to be independent and agreed. I was the first one to enter my homeroom class. I sat patiently in my seat until the teacher arrived.

"Good Morning, Ahmir. Nice to see a student eager to get to class in the mornings," she smiled. I smiled back and buried my head in a book, slightly embarrassed. As the students wandered in one by one, I inspected each of them covertly trying to decide which ones would be one of the two new people I would meet today. I made eye contact with one guy about my size who nodded in my direction. I nodded back and nonchalantly said, "Hey." I noticed that most of the students don't say 'hello', but 'hey' when they greet each other. When the bell rang and we began to scramble to our next class, I casually made my way over to the boy who had nodded in my direction earlier.

"My name is, Ahmir. Nice to meet you, man," as I extended my hand towards the boy.

"Mike Kessler. Nice to meet you too," he said, as he shook my hand quickly.

"I think we have the same physics class," I said.

"Yea, I think we do. Where are you from, Ahmir?"

"Saudi Arabia. I'm living with my aunt here and wanted to go to school here for a year, before I decide if I want to attend college in the States."

JOY IN REVIVAL

"Cool," said Mike. As we walked down the hall, many people who passed us made it a point to speak to Mike. It was as if he were a local celebrity.

"You know a lot of people here, I see."

"Yeah, I've known most of these kids since middle school. It must be hard for you leaving all your friends for your last year of high school."

"We DM and chat pretty regularly, so it's not that bad," I said.

It turned out that Mike and I had a lot of the same classes. He invited me to sit with him at lunch and I met another five or six people through him. He was relatively easy to talk to, although there was something about him that intuitively made me think he was covering up a deeper sadness. On the way home, I saw Luke on the bus and sat down next to him.

"I see you're making your way around pretty well now with Mike," he said.

"I don't remember seeing you today," I said.

"I passed you a couple of times in the hall, but most times you were surrounded by the entourage that follows Mike," he said with a smirk.

"He does know a lot of people, huh?" I said.

"Well his family is very well known in this community and most people try to suck up to him for favors. That's got to be miserable. It would make me suspicious of people's motives for being my friend," Luke said.

INTRODUCING JOY

"Yeah I guess you're right," I said.

"Where do you live, Ahmir? We must be in the same vicinity, since we ride the same bus. Do you want to come over sometimes?"

"We live in Magnolia. Thanks for the invite. Let me check to see if my aunt has any plans and I'll call you if that's okay." I wrote Luke's number down and waved goodbye, as he got off at his stop.

What a productive day, I thought. I met Mike and six other people today, and now I have a personal invitation to hang out with Luke. I couldn't wait to tell my aunt about my day. She was happy to hear about the invitation from Luke and advised me to return home early so that I could finish my assignments before it got too late. I called Luke and found out his home was only a few blocks over. I rode my bike to Luke's house and found him outside on the grounds waiting for me. He had a beautiful home and motioned for me to come up the main drive. As I got off my bike and propped it up against the side of the house, I followed Luke into the house.

"My mom made us some snacks, if you're hungry."

"No, thanks. I ate right before I came over," I said.

"Feel like a game on the PlayStation? Your choice as my guest," said Luke.

"Sure," as I followed Luke into a large game room. As we walked down the hallway, I couldn't help but feel very welcome and comfortable with Luke. His little brother ran past us laughing as Luke's mom ran up behind us chasing her younger son.

JOY IN REVIVAL

"That's my little brother and mom. You'll meet both of them sooner or later."

"Cool," I said. After about an hour of intense gaming competition, Luke's mom entered the room with tall glasses of iced tea.

"Ahmir, this is my mom, Mrs. Barren."

"Hi, Ahmir. Nice to meet you. Feel free to call me Mrs. B, like all the other teens I know."

"Pleased to meet you, Mrs. B, and thank you for the drink."

"Have you had a chance to meet a lot of people yet?"

"Only a few at school. My aunt works long hours at the hospital, so she hasn't had a chance to meet many people herself."

"Luke, did you invite Ahmir to the Youth Explosion sponsored by the church in a few weeks?" Before Luke could say no, I blurted out, "I don't go to church, Mrs. B. I am an atheist and don't believe in God." There was dead silence for about twenty seconds before Luke chimed in, "I didn't invite him yet mom, but you are welcome to come, Ahmir. Just because you don't believe in God doesn't mean you can't have some fun, does it?" Following her son's que, Mrs. B immediately extended the invitation to come and enjoy the games, music and great food.

"It's not like I have a full schedule, but I will check with my aunt and let you know if that's okay?"

For the rest of my visit, I got to know Luke pretty well and even played catch with his little brother for a while.

INTRODUCING JOY

His family seemed very nice and really made me feel at home. That evening I told my aunt about my experience at the Barren's. My aunt was raised in the Muslim faith, as was my entire family, although she was not a practicing Muslim. I found it odd that she was not too pleased to hear that I declared myself an atheist.

"Do you want to attend this function at their church? What faith are the Barrens by the way?"

"Luke says they are Christians and if the others are like his family, I think I will have a good time. It's not like I am going to get converted or join their fellowship."

"This is your call, Ahmir. Just let me know if you feel pressured in any way."

Over the next few weeks, I met a few more people and had lunch with Mike regularly. Luke and I hung out after school at least twice per week. He met my aunt and she seemed to like Luke and support our friendship.

"What are your plans this weekend?" I asked Mike.

"My parents are going away for the weekend to some resort, so I am on my own. I haven't decided to do anything yet. What about you?"

"Well, Luke Barren and his family have asked me to come to a Youth Explosion sponsored by their church. It sounds fun, so I think I will hang out with them," I said.

"I did not figure you as a 'Holy-roller', Ahmir," Mike quipped.

JOY IN REVIVAL

"What's a 'Holy-roller'? I am not familiar with that term," I said.

"You know, a church boy. The kind that preach Jesus and damn all of us to hell who don't live up to their standards." I sensed Mike felt very hostile and defensive.

"I don't believe in God, Mike. My family is Muslim, and I choose not to believe in Jesus, Allah, Buddha, or any god. Luke has never pressured me, and we don't even talk religion. He is just a cool guy to hang out with. I didn't mean to offend you."

"I apologize for pre-judging you. I am like you, man. I don't believe in any of it either. My family call themselves Catholics, but we never go to church, unless my father is closing a big deal and his client is religious. Then we suddenly put on a dog and pony show and mysteriously show up at the same church as his client. It is all political anyway."

"That is an interesting view," I said, as I changed the subject.

Saturday morning Luke and his family were scheduled to pick me up. I was actually looking forward to hanging out with his family. I thought of Mike sitting home alone and felt sorry for him. With all the peers who flocked around him, he really did choose to be more of a loner. My aunt came out to meet the Barren family when they pulled up to the house. Mrs. B was very cordial and extended the invitation for my aunt to join us. My aunt politely declined, as she had recently arrived home after working twelve hours. When we drove on the fairgrounds, it reminded me of a large carnival. There were several tents

INTRODUCING JOY

set up and rides for the smaller children. Luke and I headed towards the basketball court where a game was being played. Mrs. B and Luke's brother headed towards one of the tents. Luke explained to me that this event was not only for members of his church, but several churches in the Metropolitan area, open to everyone. As the basketball game ended, I thought again of Mike sitting home alone.

"Do you think your mom would mind if we borrowed the car?"

"That depends on why we want to borrow it. Are you not having a good time?" Luke asked.

"Actually, it is just the opposite. I am having such a good time that I feel sorry for Mike sitting home alone. Do you think we could stop by his house and see if he would like to join us?"

"I think it is worth a try, Ahmir, but don't get your hopes up. Mike really gets defensive when you talk to him about attending church functions. I have tried for years and finally just stopped inviting him," Luke replied. Luke knew exactly where Mike lived, although we didn't have his phone number. When we drove up, we had to announce ourselves at the gate. His entire property was surrounded by a six-foot brick wall. I answered for Luke and me as Mike asked who it was over the intercom. He buzzed us through the gate and was outside of the front entry when we pulled up the driveway.

"Hey guys, what's up?" Mike quipped.

"I was having such a good time at the youth explosion, I asked Luke to bring me over to see if you wanted to hang

JOY IN REVIVAL

out with us. All sorts of people are there, and the food smelled great!"

"It really is cool, and they have added a lot of new attractions this year. Come get some food man, if nothing else," Luke chimed in. Mike smiled at both of us and dramatically put his hands behind his back as if he were handcuffed.

"I guess I am cornered. I will come, but I will drive so I can bail whenever I get ready," Mike said. We waited in the car for Mike to change and follow us back to the fairgrounds. The three of us had a great time for the rest of the afternoon. I tasted almost everything they had to offer and loved it. I got in on a soccer tournament and scored for Luke's church, while Mike and Luke teamed up and beat every contender they had on the tennis courts. At the end of the afternoon, all attendees were separated into different tents by gender and age range. Our tent was filled with boys between the ages of fifteen to nineteen. Luke explained to Mike and me that one of the youth Pastors for this conference would talk to us for a little while, and then we would be free to go.

"This sounds like my que to exit," said Mike.

"Listen, if I have to stay, you can at least stay with me seeing how much fun you had today," I said.

"I'll be happy to drop you off somewhere," quipped Mike.

"No, Luke was nice enough to invite me and I am not going to bail on him now. He said it would not last long, so hang out Mike until the end," I suggested. Mike pretended to sulk, but he walked ahead of us into the tent to find a seat. As I looked around, I noticed several guys

INTRODUCING JOY

from some of my classes. Luke's father took center stage, to my surprise.

"I trust you all have had a wonderful time and will give me a few minutes of your time to tell you about my best friend." I listened intently as Mr. B told us about his experience growing up and how he was first introduced to Jesus Christ. He was so honest and graphic, as he told his story, that I did not feel as though he was preaching to me but introducing me to a great friend in his absence. The room was completely silent other than the voice of Mr. B. The atmosphere was intense, not mournful or agitated, but mesmerized and captivated by every word Mr. B spoke. I had never experienced such a peace. At the end of Mr. B's introduction of Christ, he extended an invitation for anyone in the arena who would like to know Christ personally to come forward. Many boys went to the front of the room, where Mr. B and several other men hugged them and cried with some.

There was such an open display of pure emotion, sincerity and love. I caught the swift movement of Mike's hand, as he brushed his hand across his eyes. At that very moment, I felt warmth in my heart and a voice in my head began to speak to me.

"What you are feeling and lacking in words to describe, Ahmir, is Joy. I am a Fruit of the Spirit that comes from God. God used Mr. B today to engage and connect with those in here. Many were secretly hurting and in emotional pain, like Mike, while others like you were secretly searching for truth. In opening up your heart today to hear Mr. B's testimony, you yielded to what you heard and felt and let the Spirit of God into your heart. There are

JOY IN REVIVAL

no fireworks, the heavens did not open and shoot down trumpeting angels, but the angels are rejoicing that you now know and believe in your heart that there is a God. In your kindness and compassion towards Mike today, you received a great reward and met me. I will always reside in your heart now, along with the Holy Spirit. You will still experience sadness, sorrow, and anger at different times in your life, but as you build your spiritual relationship with God, you will learn how to embrace me even during those tough times. You found out today that only God can speak to this many people all at once and give them all exactly what they need. At the very moment, Mike let me into his heart, you felt that wall he had built up fall even in your own heart."

I knew there was no one visibly talking to me, but the conversation was as real as any I had engaged in all day. When I came out of my own deep thoughts, I realized that Mike and Luke were standing nearby weeping and hugging. Once again, Joy overwhelmed my heart as I rejoiced inwardly. There was no longer any doubt in my mind and heart that God is real.

SCRIPTURE FOR REFERENCE:

"Then shall the virgin rejoice in the dance, both young men and old together: for I will turn their mourning into joy, and will comfort them, and make them rejoice from their sorrow."

(Jeremiah 31:13 KJV)

JOYFUL QUESTION:

How can you better share your joy and the good news of Jesus Christ with non-believers?

INTRODUCING JOY

JOYFUL AFFIRMATION:

I will let my light so shine that others will be drawn to me and see the good works of Christ in me. I will be used as a mighty vessel to attract non-believers to salvation and the Body of Christ.

CHAPTER 6
JOY IN FORGIVENESS

I grew up in the Midwest on the wrong side of the tracks, some might say. I was raised by a single mother who worked long hours in a factory to provide for me and my siblings. I was the middle child out of five children. My dad decided after the fifth child that marriage and fatherhood was way too cumbersome for his freelance lifestyle. By the time I was nine, the home-again-gone-again visits stopped and my hatred towards him cemented. I promised myself never to marry or have children, so that I didn't put myself in the situation that he had. If I wanted to be a single man with no attachments, the first thing I would make sure of was not to get emotionally attached to anyone. I loved my siblings and I would do anything for my Mom except marry or give her a grandchild.

My older brothers couldn't wait to get out of Indiana, so right after high school they both enlisted in the military. My younger sisters were very protective of my Mom, as was I, so they settled down with families of their own in our small midwestern town. I wasn't that keen on making

INTRODUCING JOY

Indiana my forever home, so I decided to work hard in school and make education my way up and out. I'm not ashamed or knocking my humble beginnings, but I wanted to financially help my Mom, and I wanted so much more for myself. I earned an academic scholarship to the University of Georgia. My Mom and siblings were very proud and happy for me. I might not have had the sendoff that some college bound students would receive, but love and pride were in great supply.

During my four years at the University of Georgia (UGA), I worked two jobs and worked my butt off to keep my grade point average above the scholarship requirement. I worked on campus in the bookstore a few days per week and worked nights and weekends at a local pub on E. Broad street as a waiter. My college experience did not include wild parties, UGA football games or frat parties. I was focused on getting my degree and sending Mom a small monthly allowance to do something special for herself. The first time I sent the money she called to tell me that she had sent it back. I literally had to convince her that this was my way of thanking her for all she sacrificed for us. I lied and threatened to drop out of school if she ever returned the money again. Funny thing was she believed me and talking to my sister confirmed that Mom would treat herself every now and then.

In my senior year, I broke my own oath. I let my guard down and got emotionally attached to a local girl from Athens. Savannah was no ordinary local girl. Her father was a state representative for district 117 in Athens. I was working in the bookstore in September when this girl came in with a battery-operated cart. It was the coolest thing I

JOY IN FORGIVENESS

had ever seen. It was about three feet high and three feet wide with a collapsible handle. The handle literally guided the direction of the cart. "So, do you get paid by the hour to examine my cart, or can you direct me to a real worker who can help me fill the cart with the items I need to purchase?" she said. As I focused in on the person with this rich Southern drawl, quick wit with sarcastic undertones, a beautiful brown-eyed girl looked back at me with the cutest side smirk. "I do get paid by the hour, but I know I can't afford to tip you for your comic relief. I can help you fill that cool cart with the supplies that you need," I responded, captivated by her brown eyes and thick brown hair pulled up in a ponytail. She handed me her massive list, and I proceeded to load her cart. As she checked out, I scanned her student ID and took note of her name, Savannah Wilshire.

About a week later, I was bussing tables at the pub on a Friday night when Savannah entered with two other girls. She didn't notice me at first, but as I cleared the table adjacent to the one where she sat, she motioned for me to come over.

"Hey you! Are you trying to make all the money in Athens?" she smiled.

"As much as I can handle," I said. "Good Evening ladies. I'll send your waiter shortly."

"Why not earn this tip and take our order while you're here?" she quipped. "I'd be happy to Ms. Wilshire."

"Well, well, well. Someone gets extra credit points for knowing my name. Now who might you be, Mr. Moneybags?" she smiled.

INTRODUCING JOY

"My apologies, I am Terrence Kessler. And by the way, your name was on your student ID when I charged your items in the bookstore to your account." Her girlfriends laughed as I walked away from the table with their order. This was the beginning of my first serious relationship in twenty-two years.

Savannah was a freshman majoring in Political Science. She had political aspirations like her father, but after her sophomore year in college, she changed her major to Pre-Law. She decided that she preferred to judicate the law, rather than create it. Dating Savannah had a huge influence on me and is what persuaded me to stay at UGA for two additional years to earn my MBA in International Business. During the first year of our relationship, it was hard for me to relate to Savannah having this massive estate during the summer to herself, with the exception of a two-week trip somewhere overseas with her girlfriends. I finally met her parents during a reelection event for her dad when he returned to Athens during a Thanksgiving break.

My introduction could hardly be characterized as warm and fuzzy. He shook my hand and looked right past me, as if I were a committed voter that he need not spend much time on. The emotions invoked by this brief encounter stirred up something in me. I remember when I was about eight years old, the softball team I was on won the division championship. I had made a major play in the game and couldn't wait to tell Dad about it. I barely waited for the car to be put into park, before I jumped out. Running to the front door I burst into the house calling out to my Dad. Annoyed, Dad waved me away as he was on a phone call. I waited attentively asserting my stance that I

JOY IN FORGIVENESS

wasn't leaving. I remembered he put the phone aside for a moment and said, "What's so important Terrence?" As I began to recount the highlights of my amazing play, he interrupted me and said, "Is that all?" Those three words made me feel dismissed, insignificant and irrelevant in my Dad's life. Savannah's mom was more attentive and asked me about my parents and aspirations. When I began to tell her that my Mom was divorced and worked hard to raise five children by herself, it was very evident that Mrs. Wilshire lost the enthusiasm to continue the conversation. "They treat everyone that way, Terrence. Don't put too much stock into their first impression. Once they get to know you, you might hold their attention for five full minutes," she joked. I smiled and hugged her, as we moved on to another area to join some mutual friends. I felt dismissed and judged. In my mind, I would have to earn their respect to prove that I was worthy of dating their daughter. It irritated me that I felt this vulnerable, but when Savannah smiled as she walked towards me, that feeling was immediately replaced with love.

We married despite her parents' disapproval and settled in Atlanta after Savannah finished law school. Over the next ten years, I climbed the corporate ladder as an international investment banker, while Savannah worked hard in a prominent law firm in Atlanta. I loved our life together. We were equally ambitious, although I'm sure our motives and drive came from two very different places. My family adored Savannah and we made sure to schedule Mother's Day weekends in Indiana annually. This was my one non-negotiable and Savannah agreed since her Mom claimed Christmas eve and day. Savannah announced prior

INTRODUCING JOY

to our trip to Indiana one year that she was pregnant. My response showed that I was more startled than thrilled. *Fatherhood?* Fear consumed my thoughts for a split second. I don't know how to be a father. My own father-in-law barely spent any quality time with Savannah, since the day I met him. I hear that my brothers are great fathers, but they live overseas and are away from their families for a large part of the year. *What example do I have?* Loving Savannah is one thing, *but fatherhood...*

When our son Michael was finally born, I took two weeks off to adjust to this life changing event. Savannah hired a nanny, and we made sure Michael wanted for nothing. We both loved our son, but we had an established lifestyle with a few more rungs on our professional ladder to climb. Once we reached our personal pinnacle, we would give our son our full attention. The younger years were manageable. Children are self-absorbed, so you give them what they want, and everyone is happy. Savannah made most of the schedule allowances to ensure she was home to have supper with Michael every night. I committed to travel less internationally for the first four years, but once Michael began school, I changed my commitment to be home by Saturday morning if I was away on business. Savannah enrolled Michael in all types of extra-curricular activities. She felt that he should be exposed to all choices and then allow his natural abilities and interests determine which activity he would commit to. Initially Michael loved Tee-ball, then softball. It wasn't intentional, but I realized in hindsight, that I barely attended any of Michael's games. If I got in early Saturday morning, the jet lag usually rendered me comatose for the next eight to twelve hours. As an afflu-

JOY IN FORGIVENESS

ent couple in Atlanta, all of Michael's peers were attending boarding school for middle and high school instruction. Savannah and I blindly followed the crowd and assumed we were doing the right thing when we enrolled Michael at the same school most of his classmates would attend. It never occurred to us to ask Michael what he wanted, and he never stated that he didn't want to attend. Michael appeared to love boarding school for the first two years. That all changed around the age of thirteen. To be honest, Savannah and I both resumed our kid-free lifestyle and began to miss family events at Michael's school. We picked him up for major holidays, but made too many apologies regarding family weekend, awards programs, and other schoolwide events. Michael began getting into trouble and even kicked out of one of the finest boarding schools in Tennessee. We sent him to a therapist and threatened to take away privileges. He convinced us to enroll him at a local private school and the therapist agreed that being at home with Savannah regularly would benefit Michael and our family dynamics. Michael submitted to following the rules at school and at home. The unfortunate thing that developed over the next few years was a distance between he and I. He didn't exhibit anger towards me, but our encounters alone, made those old feelings of dismissal and irrelevance come up that my Dad and Senator Wilshire provoked years earlier. I wanted to reach my son, but I didn't know how. I was too proud to ask for help or to tear down my own wall of fear.

I returned home from an overseas meeting one Saturday afternoon to find Savannah gone to visit her Mom in

INTRODUCING JOY

Athens. I remember looking for Michael and finding the house empty. I awoke about three hours later when I heard the door chime. "Michael, is that you?" I called out. No one answered, so I got up to see who had entered.

"Michael, did you hear me. What's going on, son?" I asked.

"Hey, Dad. Sorry I didn't hear you. I'm just getting in from an event with some friends. How long are you here for?" asked Michael.

"A few weeks, I hope. I just got in from Japan, so I was napping until I heard you come in."

"Dad can I ask you something?"

"Yes," I said.

"Do you believe in God?" asked Michael.

"Wow, where is this coming from?" I asked.

"I went to a church event today with Luke and a new friend, and I think I experienced the presence of God there. Dad, I have been sad for so many years of my life and blamed you and Mom for my unhappiness. Today, I realized that it wasn't all your fault, but I didn't know how to express to you what I was feeling or what I needed to feel better. I now know that I was lonely and felt unloved and unwanted. Today, I found out that God loves me, always has and always will. I know that I'm never alone, because He will be with me, always. I really want to apologize for my actions over the years and let you know that I love you and Mom."

JOY IN FORGIVENESS

My heart was about to explode! I couldn't do this right now. I put my hand over my heart and tapped it as an expression of mutual love, as I quickly left the room. I was incapable of responding at this time. I put on some shoes and grabbed my keys. I needed to be alone to process what had just happened. I found myself driving aimlessly up and down Interstate 85, until I finally pulled off at an exit and parked on a quiet street.

"My God! My seventeen-year-old son apologized to me for my misbehavior. God, I don't know what to call this that I'm feeling. Yes, I do. It's guilt, remorse and shame. God, please help me! I don't want to lose my son. Please forgive me." I cried out as I sobbed.

"He already has, Terrence. My name is Joy, and I am a Fruit of the Holy Spirit. God knew this day would come when you would surrender to Him and allow Him to strengthen and heal your soul. I know you can't see me, but what you are hearing is coming from within you, and I am very real. I met your son earlier today, and it was his encounter with God that strengthened him to pour out his heart to you. Terrence, it was the unforgiveness that you held against your own father that erected the wall in your heart towards Michael. You thought it would be easier to not build a relationship and disappoint Michael than it would be to build a loving relationship and fail. Michael's forgiveness towards you allows you to forgive your father and repair your relationship with your son. God loves us so deeply that He gave his only begotten son, Jesus, to suffer and die for mankind. The example you were desiring for all these years could always be found in God the Father. Our Father in Heaven loves us unconditionally. That

INTRODUCING JOY

love is available to you and every human being who recognizes and accepts his son Jesus as Lord of their life. This is your opportunity, Terrence, to be free and made whole."

"Yes, God I do believe you love me and only you could bring my son to me. Help me, Lord, to follow your example and love my son completely," Terrence wept. The peace that rested on Terrence after hours of self-reflection and prayer, allowed him to return home as a new creature in Christ. Terrence embraced his son and apologized for his own shortcomings and unforgiveness. Although he might never have the courage to contact his own father, he had forgiven him, which released him from that bondage. His new relationship with Christ and Michael were now paramount in his life.

SCRIPTURE FOR REFERENCE:

"And, ye fathers, provoke not your children to wrath; but bring them up in the nurture and admonition of the Lord."

(Ephesians 6:4 KJV)

JOYFUL QUESTION:

How can you practice forgiveness more in your own life? How have you seen unforgiveness manifest in negative ways in your life?

The root of resentment can be caused by feelings of being undervalued, dismissed or taken advantage of, etc. Do you harbor feelings of resentment? Will you acknowledge those feelings and submit them to the Lord for healing?

JOY IN FORGIVENESS

JOYFUL AFFIRMATION:

Today, I exercise the power that is within me to forgive myself and others who have hurt or offended me. I walk in this forgiveness every day, and as a result, good fruit is yielded in my life, including the Fruit of the Spirit.

EPILOGUE

Each of you reading this book will encounter me at some point in your life. Many of you might have already, and I will be the first to 'Rejoice' with you. There is no one exempt from the joy of the Lord. Not every encounter with me is a result of an emotional breakdown or crisis. God is omniscient; He knows everything. His wisdom and knowledge determines my introduction, both when it is time and to who. There is no situation or deed that is done which will disqualify a willing soul from receiving the Fruit of the Spirit. There are nine of us in all, Love, Peace, Patience (long suffering), Gentleness, Goodness (kindness), Faith, Meekness, Temperance, and me, Joy. Each of us have unique characteristics and functions. You can read Galatians chapter 5 to get a biblical perspective of the Fruit of the Spirit. Petition God in prayer about who you can share this book with. It would be my pleasure to meet them. This Joy that you have, the world didn't give it and the world can't take it away!

To order additional copies of

INTRODUCING JOY
EVIDENCE OF VICTORY
FROM THE INSIDE OUT

visit Amazon at www.amazon.com
or
visit your local bookstore

Email Carol Spear at:
honored2write@gmail.com

www.ingramcontent.com/pod-product-compliance
Lightning Source LLC
Chambersburg PA
CBHW061503040426
42450CB00008B/1465